Origami Doll

New and Collected Poems

Shirley McClure in Boyle, County Roscommon
photo by Catherine Gundry-Beck

Shirley McClure

ORIGAMI DOLL

New and Collected Poems

Edited by Jane Clarke

Origami Doll:
New and Collected Poems

is published in 2019 by
ARLEN HOUSE
42 Grange Abbey Road
Baldoyle
Dublin 13
Ireland
Phone: +353 86 8360236
Email: arlenhouse@gmail.com

978–1–85132–210–7, paperback

International distribution by
SYRACUSE UNIVERSITY PRESS
621 Skytop Road, Suite 110
Syracuse,
New York
USA 13244–5290
Phone: 315–443–5534/Fax: 315–443–5545
Email: supress@syr.edu
www.syracuseuniversitypress.syr.edu

Typesetting by Arlen House

Cover artwork by Catherine Gundry-Beck

Contents

Preface

After Shirley McClure's untimely death from cancer in September 2016 her publisher, Alan Hayes of Arlen House, invited me to edit a *New & Collected Shirley McClure*. It's my honour to present *Origami Doll: New and Collected Poems,* which includes Shirley's two published collections, *Stone Dress* (Arlen House, 2015) and *Who's Counting?* (Bradshaw Books, 2010) as well as the new poems, collectively entitled *Origami Doll,* which Shirley completed shortly before her death, and which are published here in book form for the first time.

Shirley McClure's poems are distinguished by her unique interplay of humour and poignancy, ebullience and restraint, sassiness and tenderness. Her lines display her finely attuned musical ear and her meticulous attention to rhythm and internal rhyme. She gives us poems to accompany us through the pain and joy of being human; poems that are courageous in facing suffering and loss, compassionate in reflecting our responses and celebratory in showing how love and hope persist.

Special thanks to Shirley's husband, Philip Beck, for his painstaking work collecting her new poems and for his help and support in the preparation of this book. Geraldine Mitchell provided invaluable editorial support and encouragement. Thanks also to Eithne Hand, Jessica Traynor, Michaela Wright and Katie Donovan. My gratitude to Shirley's family and friends, and in particular Roger and Rhona. And finally to Eina McHugh for her creative guidance and to Alan Hayes for his commitment to this publication.

Jane Clarke
February 2019

ORIGAMI DOLL

New and Collected Poems

ORIGAMI DOLL

Sweet Apples

Say you owned a house
with one tree in the garden

and from that tree toppled
the most aromatic apples in town,

would you allow those apples
to rot on the grass, make food

for the jackdaws that worried
your cat, or would you cook up

strudels, pies, sauces,
drink cider as the snow fell

on the abiding branches
of your only tree?

Origami Doll

Alone
on a mirrored shelf
she displays

her flat chest,
the artful grace
of her kimono.

So cleverly made
you'll never
work her out.

Tentatively passed
from hand to hand,
she's kept away

from forces
that will change her
into ash or mâché.

But as you know,
a doll
has a mind of her own –

she's in love
with the illusion
of flying.

No matter how
careful you are,
one day

without so much
as a bow,
she will leave you

for the River of
Three Crossings
or you may find her

dressed in white,
six coins in the palm
of her hand.

HUARAZ

It was dark when we got there,
glad to be met at the bus stop,

two narrow beds and a weight
of alpaca blankets to slow us to sleep.

In the morning our smiling señora
led us into her garden, pointed upwards.

No! How could we have slept
unaware of the Cordillera Blanca,

its snow-poncho'd vastness?
As if she understood,

she served us chamomile tea,
blossoms floating;

that taste and the breath
of the Andes, forever joined.

APHRODITE MOMENT

Because he puts Adonis in the shade,
such curls, such shoulders,
arms to draw you in;
and murmurs *darling,* not because
he doesn't know your name;

what harm to thread
those locks between your fingers,
roll those muscles underneath your thumbs
and hear him sigh,
like the ocean washing stones.

For a Dress

after John William Waterhouse's 'The Lady of Shalott Looking at Lancelot', *1894*

This your idea of a joke, John?

You give me a dress
I can wear to Seáno's debs,

then make me stand in this,
like, ri*dic*ulous position,

bent over like I'm waiting
for some mad ugly artist
to *ride* me –

oh I got you
there,

and after – don't you
dare Facebook this bit –

you tie my fuckin' knees up
with gold rope?

Some 'Lady' –
you can keep her.

One Night Stand

Notwithstanding
the foregoing,
it's foregone
but not forgotten.

You're for going,
I'm for standing.
I'm not standing
for your going

but you're going
notwithstanding.
You're forgetting
the foregoing.

I can't stand it
that you're going.
I'm on standby
without knowing

why you're going
going, going
notwithstanding
the foregoing.

A Spanish Affair

He chooses free range eggs
at Tesco, garlic, potatoes
and the closest he can find
to *cebolla española*, because
tonight he's gonna show ya
his *tortilla española* – with
some excellent wine.

His bountiful swag –
one on each handlebar,
he carries the bags.
You shout, '*Cuidado con el vino –*
que caro y que fino!' But
he hasn't even seen you
as the plastic snags

and the passionate Rioja
comes crashing – green glass
shattered, wine on the ground.
He throws down his bike,
flings his hands in the air,
back into Tesco
with a big Spanish swear.

He emerges with a second
which falls as if it's destined.
'*Jota y joder*!'
Three times it happens:
his deep dark frown,
green glass shattered,
wine on the ground.

Ecdysis

All reptiles shed their skins, referred to as ecdysis [...] In general, snakes will slough at least once a month – Drs Foster & Smith

At Weight Watchers
this week's speaker
is a stylist, so for once
we don't all turn up in leggings;
there are attempts at florals,
lipstick, infinity scarves.

But when she starts to speak,
this Medusa with braids
that are purely there to lure us
down the sine waves
of her perfect form,
we know we're wasting our time.

Purge your wardrobe, she gushes,
keep nothing that isn't a cosy fit,
believe me, you'll feel freer.

We don't believe her,
because we know those jeans
that were right last March,
but too baggy in April,
then too clingy for the beer garden
on August nights,

too loose at Halloween,
too tight on Christmas Eve
will be right again – one day.

You Stayed On

I left the party early. Already
it was getting out of hand.
One woman liked to shake
her breasts about – they were
long and dislikeably white,
with nipples like rose hips
that butted at the other dancers
in the dangerous light.

Loud laughter woke me,
you'd brought the party back.
Through the wall the talk
was all about the kissing game.
I listened closer, heard how
they'd passed liquor
mouth to mouth, screeching
as they listed names.

I knew you'd taken part,
I even knew whose lips
you'd tasted – that streel
with the tubular breasts,
yes hers, and so I shouted
I can hear you! And the whole
house fell silent.

Another Busy Weekend for the *Snow White* Cast

Snow White has been practising
kissing the Handsome Prince.
She must ensure that, in spite of
the pressure from his parting lips,

tease of his mintiness,
point of irresistibility, moment of relenting –
her blood-red lipstick will remain unstained,
she must awaken perfect.

This requires practice, and practise she will,
chaise-longued back-stage in her Ugg Boots,
her pink lacy tights and short shorts; a luminous top
that shows her milk-white belly, button hooped by a ring.

There's a tongue-ring too,
which the director has noticed:
Now Snow White, she cries, *Enunciate!*
It's Hand-some Prince, not Han-Thumb Printh!

They practise, coy hand on coy hand,
his eyes on the stillness of her chest,
till finally on Sunday afternoon,
as if he has lost hope of her ever reviving,

he tunnels in,
a fox finding his den;
delving inside her until,
like a half-buried person,

she must suddenly heave, gasp,
enliven her manicured fingers,
reach for his shoulders;
her blood-red lipstick forgotten.

Georgie

Once she got the knack of automatic writing
it was as if she'd leapt into a river in full spate;
spluttering at first, the words came out in Latin
or Italian, and the hand was bad, almost illegible.

Like a moorhen she tuned into where was safe
for nesting. She predicted their first conception.
Not so mysterious, the gossips whispered,
when the cock flew further down the bank,

his chest puffed up with lust and magic.
He'll be back, she forecast, as sure as summer
drought will tame the river, have it crying out
for rain, for rain.

Astrogeography

Is it my fate or fortune
to inhabit a grey terraced house
in just this part of Bray?

Is my soul attuned
to this one spot,
or has it more to do with practicalities:

proximity to urban population,
price of property, *and sure you're here now,*
so why would you move?

The astrology of place
can pin-point on a map
your best latitude and longitude,

your prime location,
your front seat
under the stars.

What if Saturn in a square
to the mid-heaven, or Venus on the cusp
would have me camping

in the Hindu Kush,
or park me in a trailer
in Wyoming?

If the Moon on the ascendant
would base me in a convent
in Toledo,

should I not book my ticket now,
become a life-time member
of the eternal fringe?

Bookmark

be my space-keeper
hard-wearing reliable
beautiful thing

save my place
and you may rest
on my soft lap

as I progress
through episodes
day-dream

past the chapters
nibble at
your borders

be prepared
for silent times
for years on end

when all the stories
are of betrayal
all the poems

drench you
in my sad
sad rain

and in return
what you love best
all night each night

enfolded
in the centre-fold
your place

my place
in the body
of words

HOW TO BE A BEAD CURTAIN

after Jeet Thayil

Get leggy. Wrap your thighs
around anyone who's passing.

Cling on for that extra moment
to shoulders that resist you.

Stretch one long limb
the length of someone's shadow.

Drop abruptly
down the seam of her sun-dress.

Quick, lick her ankle,
breathe.

Lesbos

No longer famous
for its naked women

smoking hash
and chatting one another up,

two fingers to the Peeping Toms
who can't believe their seedy luck.

Kids don't start to giggle
when they hear the name

and we don't think of Sappho
on her sunbed, her pen dipped

in seagull ink. We've grown
tolerant, passed laws for the gays.

We holiday in Spain now,
Greece has grown too hot,

its beaches not as smart
as those on the Costa Blanca.

Farewell to Politics

I don't go to meetings any more
to argue or agree or take the minutes.

I don't keep Tuesday evenings free
for local branch,

Thursdays for sub-committees,
Saturdays for marches.

I don't miss squatting at the US Embassy
or canvassing Rathmines,

that moment when I ring the doorbell,
ready for a brush-off or a full-scale row.

I don't miss writing policies, imagining
a perfect world for bees

and trees and sheep and women.
That time they shoved me on a podium

with reps from all the other parties
comes back to me in nightmares,

the mercy in the Fianna Fáiler's eyes,
the walnut in my throat.

I don't miss all the effort that's required
to change the world, but can I trust

and is it fair to think
that someone else will do it?

HOMELESS MAN FOUND DEAD IN DOORWAY

Maybe she's measuring out porridge oats
in the silence of the house, lighting
the gas, when the doorbell rings.

Still in her dressing-gown, she hesitates,
adds water, turns the dial low. Or maybe
she's dressed already, sweeping away crumbs,

her mind on this afternoon's appointment,
the presents she'll buy down the town. The list
is somewhere, *now where did I leave it?*

When she opens the chain-locked front door
two men are standing on her step,
hoodies and hats against the morning freeze.

They're apologising, and she doesn't know why;
cars rumble past and the wind distorts their words.
If you had a recent photo, maybe with the family?

When she closes the door the phone is ringing,
a burning smell floats out from the kitchen,
and on the hall table – there's the Christmas list.

Deep Sleep

1

Don't remind me
of the child so fast asleep.
He slept thus in my womb
a sleep so deep.

2

I wrenched him from sleep
from all that he loved,
and now he's gone back
to sleep on me again.

3

His forehead is still
and soft his pulses beat.
His body is fish,
two shellfish his feet.

4

The dew must come in sleep
for it damps his brow.
In sleep there must be music
for it rocks him now.

5

Smooth as running water
stirs his quiet breath,
his eyelids flutter
like a laurel leaf.

6

Do not disturb him
so good, and so fine,
until he awakens
of his will, not mine ...

7

Sleep helped by roof and door
these simple things and human;
the earth which is our mother
his mother who is woman.

8

Let's see if I can learn
to sleep as once I did
for now I've learnt too well
disloyal wakefulness.

9

So let us to sleep,
and may we not awake,
this short sleep is granted
until the dawn-break.

Gabriela Mistral
Translation: Shirley McClure

A Daughter

She'd done this before;
blood was commonplace.

A boy, then one or two
who lost their bearings.

But my mother made it
with me.

When he saw me, after
the clenching, the expulsion,

after I'd squeezed through
the crimson door of my life,

he beamed, *I've got a daughter!*
I watched, nonplussed

from my basket of white,
dizzy, bruised, but open

to persuasion. Who was
this blue-eyed man

who rubbed
his hands together,

lit a cigarette
and kissed my mother?

I was here now,
things would change.

Seven Miles

The day I ride my bike to Callan
is my first time out alone
along the tarmac roads.

Warm enough for Airtex,
I've ten coins in my purse,
a sandwich in my pannier.

A downhill dash,
brakes … whoop,
free!

Far off in Ardkeen,
my mother undergoes
a *woman's operation*.

Breathless I push up
a broken road
that sizzles in the heat.

My aunt said, *Callan,*
seven miles,
oh, you'd make it to Callan.

The tyres twick and twerr,
a constant
turning breath.

My mum's asleep,
the doctors cut away,
they didn't tell us properly.

I roll past hedges,
fields of hay,
my cream shorts blossom.

A lorry hoots,
the driver shouts,
he pauses with his load.

My bare legs lodge in nettles
till they sting
like deepest cuts inside.

DRESSING TABLE

My mother stored woollens
in the drawers,

hers gentian or olive,
his mustard, russet, brown.

A mahogany knob
replaced by one darker,

lacking the wood-swirls
of the rest.

Another remained loose
as if left like this on purpose.

I do not remember her
gazing in the mirror,

nor fixing her hair
with this antique brush.

On the embroidered tray-cloth
was her Yardley powder puff;

a leather-framed photograph
of us.

Just once, nearing the end,
we sat together on her bed.

How long will this go on?
Not long, I answered. *Oh, thank God.*

Now the dressing table
holds my clothes,

and unless it's held crooked
the knob still comes away in my hand.

In one tiny drawer
is my mother's foundation,

tan dust compacted
in its navy case, shut tight.

That Cardigan

From February
my mother wore
a coarse green cardigan.
It seemed
she was never
warm enough
to peel it off;
it held on like gum
stuck to its wrapper,
like those blue
Rhodesian stamps
glued in an album
in the attic.

Poster Girl

In the surgeons' rooms
on the first floor, Suite 3,

a poster in a wooden frame
hangs above Mr O'Mara's head,

making it hard to concentrate
as he pronounces phrases like

as a precaution we'll remove
the lymph nodes, and,

rough sailing for a year, but
most women do quite well.

It's a full-frontal photograph,
a naked woman running in a forest.

In place of her right breast
there's a tattoo – a sprig

of coloured roses crossing from
her sternum to her underarm.

Her left breast flies up
in what looks like joy.

How does that sound? he asks
and perhaps because the woman

in the picture looks so dignified,
so all there, so alive,

you nod and smile, say,
That sounds like a good plan;
thank you, doctor, for your time.

Scar

if this were all that was left

one tense bleached line
where they mended you

in time you might perceive it
as a battle-wound, a badge
of *I have lived*

you might join the Seamen's Union
drink tots of grog in the Salty Tusk
show off the faded ink of your tattoos

the ports you nested in
the Birds of Paradise that cried to you

Haiku Diary

Come to the blue chair,
breathe in, make a fist for me,
now that's a great girl.

Last time I fainted.
You're better off where
they can keep an eye on you.

Toast, yoghurt, the Host,
The Irish Times, Wigs Weekly,
out-patients' choices.

Anoint my head
with frankincense, you wise men,
make my hair grow back.

As the months go on
receptionists know your name –
three-legged black cat.

Tears in the morning:
eyelashes, almost all gone,
distort emotion.

The best side-effect
of chemotherapy
is smooth unshaven legs.

Tea from a white mug,
grooves that my fingers cling to,
marks the potter made.

Sign your life away,
says the postman, hands me his
electronic pen.

THE OCCUPATIONAL THERAPIST

sighs at the gradient of our garden path,
our lack of foresight, *we can't have you falling!*

She measures the stairs, the bath, the bed,
the lip of our door saddles, talks bungalows

and time-lines. She has me stand in the shower
in my sandals, roll off my bed fully clothed,

we're talking 'Ground Floor Living' now,
I can put you in touch

with some ramping firms,
though of course we're not allowed make referrals.

There's a waiting list for grants,
she bellows as she marches down our road,

and *oh yes, Miss McClure,*
do let me source you a commode.

What's Sexy?
for Philip

What's sexy about brie and chardonnay
for one? What's sexy about being the one

to take out the bins, take in the laundry,
write notes as the Sicilian oncologist

pronounces word for word new Latin
to the one you love?

What's sexy, anymore, about the one
you love, who tries to pull her weight

around the house but finds herself
too heavy, or the pills too light?

What's sexy are the careful notes
you take, the way your 'I' contains

a backward-looking 'S', the 'I' holds firm,
makes love in all the ways it knows.

Bray to Greystones Road

After the roundabout the road lifts:
left, Bray Head, right, the Sugarloaf,
a nest of trees, a lime-green canopy

about the car. I climb the hill, over
the top, the moment that exhilarates.
Today the sea is periwinkle,

the depth of it consumes me.
This hilltop gives up what Wordsworth
sang about, 'god's country',

what hang-gliders return to;
for seconds it is mine.
The graveyard's on the left;

my chosen resting place,
but no plots for sale. The nice man
tells me to ring again,

as he did six months ago. Nothing
has changed except my body.
There's another graveyard in Kilquade.

Get Well Soon

He was a man of habit;
same blue cardigan, *The Irish Times,*
same briefcase all four years of college,
same desk in the Lecky.

We'd sit together in the Arts Block,
mimicking professors, sharing notes
on his Friel, my MacNeice;
his North, my South.

In final year, when there was almost
no time left, he asked me to the Trinity Ball.
He was Gatsby in his bow tie,
number one was *Every Breath You Take.*

After more than thirty years, he writes,
same fountain pen, same script,
a kindness in his words: *We had*
a lot of fun back then. I won't ever forget that.

I would love this letter, if it wasn't
such an end of chapter message,
the ones that people send, in case.

Last Day

If I perch here, head shaded,
my toes in the sun;

if I focus
on the dark blue pool tiles,
the pepper tree reflected
on the water;

those terracotta steps
I never noticed till today;

if I adjust my hearing,
so the barking hound,
the belching from a man next door
are filtered out;

if I can keep just those
clacking bird songs,
the bitter chocolate taste,
the smell of lemons;

then perhaps I can allow today
to be the last day.

Midnight

Delicate, midnight.
I overhear the knots of the rose bush:
the sap pushes rising to the rose.

I hear
the scorched stripes of the regal
tiger: they do not let him sleep.

I hear
somebody's verses,
and they swell in the night
like a sand-dune.

I overhear
my mother sleeping
with two breaths.
(I sleep in her,
my fifth year).

I hear the Rhône descending
and, like a blind father of foam that is blind,
bringing me down.

And after I hear nothing
but that I'm falling
in Arlean walls –
sun-filled.

Gabriela Mistral
Translation: Shirley McClure

May God

I am searching
for a kind of god:
like ours
but feminine,

a rock,
root,
river
pan-deity

a hey girl! Pachamama

who'd be as easy
standing guard for me
within a vessel

on the dresser of our kitchen,
as in a field of sunflowers

cradling like a hammock
wrought of moss & silken twine
my battered body –

she is on her way to me, I trust
she's on her way.

STONE DRESS

(Arlen House, 2015)

Budget Night

There is nothing on TV
except cost extraction strategies,
crisis cuts and cleverality.
You and I watch budget round-ups
from the old brown couch, endure
the sounds of less and less

until like semi-state bodies
we begin to merge, your right
meets my left despite the issues
of the day, alters its position
just a fraction, introduces
tried and tested measures.

The voices from the House
grow indistinct,
the old brown couch
becomes our Chamber,
there is no stopping
this amalgamation

as preferential interests are unveiled,
this fresh alliance
plunges past our thresholds,
shakes our standard rates,
leaves core weekly entitlements
untouched.

A Marriage
after Anne Stevenson

When he gave us the biopsy results,
taut phrases gleaned from the handbook
of *How Not to Shock,*
you pretended illiteracy, made him retell
in layman's language, insisted on pictures.

Later, intact in the dark together,
I whispered, *I don't think we should marry now,*
but you repeated, *I wish we'd done it sooner,*
I wish I'd asked you sooner,
no way can you get out of this.

It was what's called an unreal time,
yet more immediate, more lived in
than the café days that followed.
You bought me blue pyjamas,
rewashed and berry-scented nightly.

At home we made delicate love,
watchful of bandages,
you allowed me to lament,
allowed me to imagine
a life with you.

Engagement

Nurse dresses the wound,
we talk hormones, oestrogen,
how the levels will drop
like water in a summer pool
that yields only a dry ring,
a glaze of salt.

She says I can swim in salt
water, now that the wound
is healing; she says to ring
if there's a problem. Oestrogen
used to be my friend. The pool
is out of bounds, but I can drop

down into the waves, swim till I drop,
crawl out covered in salt.
Sea water gathers in a pool
at my feet, and even the wound
shines. Sunbathers beam oestrogen,
and I stand, hopeless in a ring

of bare-breasted women. Can't ring
any nurse about this. Can't drop
out of the world because of oestrogen.
I change in our room, taste salt.
My sun dress won't cover the wound,
I pull on an old t-shirt, curl up by the pool.

You find me at the pool.
Still not used to your ring –
the ring came before the wound,
before the floor dropped
out of the world, before salt
baths and the war against oestrogen.

Was it the oestrogen
you fell for, or the reflecting pool,
or my image conserved in salt?
Would you rather I gave back the ring,
would you rather we dropped
the whole plan? I wound

you with questions, wound with oestrogen,
the drops I have left, run from the pool,
your ring glued to my finger with salt.

The Argument for Chemotherapy

Imagine we wanted
to knock down this wall,
says the doctor.
This pen is the hammer,
which represents the tablets.

And he begins to
tap tap tap
with his ball-point pen
on the cool white wall
beside his desk.

I wonder who's next door,
an intern with a headache
or another imagistic doctor,
rapping for *her* patients' benefit
on the opposite side,

till one day,
many demonstrations
down the road,
a keyhole of hope
is exposed.

Eventually,
he rests his silver biro
on my case notes, *we would*
break down the wall.
But what if, and he stands,

I took a sledgehammer?
He swipes with tailored jacket arms,
a Victorian High Striker, a Thor:
Now you see what happens
to the wall?

Photo Shoot

Standing topless in the black box,
I pull my tummy in and hold my number up,
the hospital photographer makes pictures
of my newly-pinked right nipple.

Nurses rave about the handiwork,
scars are praised,
micro-pigmentation applauded,
yours is the best we've taken.

Never has my breast received so much attention,
maybe someday it will grace the pages
of *Plasthetics* magazine.
There is more than one way to find fame.

Specialists

Driving to St James's in a thunderstorm –
at the canal there's a new pink sign:

Hand and Foot Spa. Terms like callus peel,
gel overlay, make me wince.

At the Breast Clinic, a nurse I haven't seen
for a year examines me. *Ah yes,* she smiles,

I remember your scar: how it ends
in a V there under the axilla.

He was proud of that. I recall the surgeon
unveiling his signature finish

to a group of students. *Funny,* says the nurse,
what makes some people tick.

Missing Parts

That Easter holidays my father
had his thin, stained teeth forked out.
He had to learn to speak and eat again
before the summer term,

all with a plastic cart in his mouth.
I could not see ahead, I almost died
when one of the boys in my class asked:
'What's up with your dad? He's talking funny'.

Now me, in flimsy pink pyjamas –
heaviest thing I can bear –
unable to conceal the sudden flatness
of the right side of my chest.

A colleague visits me in hospital.
I have been coping without mirrors,
I'm not ready for him yet,
his eyes fast-tracking from my face

to the small roundness of a bandage
not making up for the fullness on my left.
His shocked male stare
like a schoolboy, reading me.

Aptitude Test

Turn left; no, right; no, left;
I prompt him as,
never great at telling
the difference,
I am doubly, no, trebly confused
by these wrong-sided cars,
these back-to-front highways,
these schematic maps.

In psychometric tests
I score poorly
on spatial awareness;
and the only thing worse,
at a party, than someone
outlining the stages of a recipe –
no pen or paper, no way
I'll remember –
are helpful directions like:
turn right after the cast-iron railings;
eighteenth bungalow on the same side
as the church. You'll see
my car outside,
you know, the Skoda ...

The funny thing is,
since the mastectomy,
despite numbness, lopsidedness
and scars, I sometimes forget
which side it was,
really forget inside my body,
not simply the words in my head
for right; no, left; no, right.

Stone Dress

Her whole body was covered with a skin hard as rock.
She was sometimes called Stone-dress.
– The Spear-Finger, Cherokee myth

When she lay by the pool,
her children would hopscotch along her,

chalking her body from one to home,
giggle as they landed

on the pebbles of her kneecaps,
the limestone of her chest.

When she baked fruitcake,
standing in her apron by the oven,

her thighs and her belly would heat
to a hundred degrees;

so when the book club arrived,
they would peel off their scarves

and their cashmere cardigans,
their knee-high boots and their skirts.

By the time they had analysed the plot,
knocked back the wine and cake,

they were all sitting naked
in the peppery room.

This was where she felt safest,
in the landscape of their folds and scars;

no jokes about her hard neck, thick skin,
here in the stone circle of her friends.

Labels

The woman ahead of me
in the queue for Customer Services
at the Bank of Ireland
has folded up her copper high-lit hair

so you can read
the Gothic characters sunk in
to the fair skin and fat that mask
her first thoracic vertebra:

splayed out between
the curve of neck and rim
of her black t-shirt – Robbie,
just where a label would be.

I think of Robbie, cushioned
by the bolster of her back, intact
in his indelibility, and wonder
has he, too, absorbed

this lover's name –
Shania, Sasha or Sinéad –
under the hood
of his Quiksilver hoodie?

Or has he a line
of Limited Edition lovers
scattered over Dublin, each one
bearing his brand?

GROOMED

Today she has been clipped, primped, squeezed,
handed back with a pink bow. She's a smooth black angel
beneath whose sleek chops, butter wouldn't melt.

Tonight is warm, the garden wild with possibility.
Suddenly the bellows of her belly surge, her body spasms
to expel the rare meat struggling in her mouth.

On the grass the hedgehog still breathes, but somehow
she has opened him, got right in without incurring
a single spine on her perfectly-barbered snout.

PROPOSAL

I don't suppose you'd marry me,
says the painter, as I draw circles
with his shoulder, trace a curving channel
from the shade of his axilla
to the rimple at his wrist.

Proposals in this job are rare.
There are the guys who whisper:
Squeeze my arches and I'll give you
anything you want; and the chancers:
groin strain; bother with me glutes.

But most men know this is worth
lying down for, staying still for.
My cook friend gets asked all the time,
guys fall in love with her Spicy Aioli;
she takes it with a pinch of salt.

When he is healed, the artist
presents me with a painting: Slea Head
in the background; the foreground, he admits,
is fantastical: a jungle-fringed path;
a young woman, hand on her Panama hat,

the other holding that of a child.
He tells me the woman is me,
the girl my niece – he's invented a niece –
both slim as Guinea grass, they gaze out
at an impossible ocean.

After the Massage

On a good day
a country woman
kisses my fingers.
These hands, she hallows,
God bless these hands.

My plainsong palms
lie holy in her grasp;
choir girl thumbs
blink, blush, swell,
Is she talking about us?

The Driving Instructor

He was a man you wouldn't ordinarily
invite into your car.

Caress the gear stick, love,
imagine it's the boyfriend.

She wished she'd put her foot down
on the ABC of feminist first principles,

charged him to keep his chevrons
on his sleeve,

but stuck in his box junction,
she daren't let the lever leave her grasp.

She should have scorched the tyres
on the acutest hairpins of revenge

or done a *Thelma and Louise,*
ignoring contra-flows and *Danger – Cliffs.*

She should have leveled all his crossings,
made him yield at the first junction,

she should have told him: *Stop –*
this is my girlfriend's car.

On Reading Two Poets

The prescribed text
presses forward its full chest
of complicated verses,
a proud half-smile

on its scarcely-opened lips,
confident that if I give it time,
read up on the Romans
– Wikipedia at least –

I too will be Pulitzered,
by the associative, sonic
and formal properties rustling
beyond mere denotation.

Instead I'm reading you,
page after naked page
swallowing your poems,
wiping their juices

from the edges of my mouth,
asking myself,
is there something wrong
if it's easy?

The Kiss

I could have been
a better student – learned Lorca
from the library stacks,

not lying
on the shag rug
in the lecturer's flat.

I half-listened to his *Verde,*
que te quiero verde,
knowing he would kiss me later;

half-believing that his tongue –
its twist and roll
around my own –

would transmit linguistics,
short-cut me
to fluency.

Exchange

I made him potluck curries,
masala-spicy with a twist of lime
when it seemed he was not going home.

He made me a walnut mantel,
a place for glass to show its colours
over the wood-burning stove.

I made him laugh,
flattered the flick of his chisel,
the burn of his saw.

He made his mark –
his mark was everywhere – this part,
believe me, I did not make up.

He fashioned a partition,
two rooms from one;
he made his side, I made mine.

Roll Up

Coiled up inside
his new wife

with her high-wire hips
and greasepaint

is a girl – or boy – baby
with hands like his,

hands that could be turned
to anything,

jelly hands turned
to mama still, holding on

for the trapeze act
of a lifetime.

I do not envy her
the canvas stretched

over the Big Top
of her being,

nor the impatient bucking
of its key performer. Once,

I would have entertained
an acrobat or lion tamer,

worn my lips red
and my neckline low

to be somebody
in that ringmaster's show.

Maternity

I want to have poems
by Caesarean section
wearing my Infallible lip gloss

and counting on my designer
obstetrician.
I will keep my bump discreet,

drink litres of San Pellegrino,
strive to avoid *striae gravidarum,*
laser them later if it comes to it.

I want to live a normal life
despite the media,
and when it's time,

my lines will glide out raring
to open their lungs and wail
as true as any natural birth.

Japanese Garden

If I'd been a garden
I'd have put down
in Japan,
relished the tickle
of a rake at sunrise,
explained myself
in circles formed in stone.

I'd have been bamboo
and lanterns,
gravel made to look
like water,
full-moon maples
extending
their baby's hands.

Why

A thoughtful guy, Why,
the kind who can't sit easy
for quizzes and queries puzzling his brow.

How was his childhood sweetheart.
They made out behind the question marks at school.
All the kids knew How and Why.

He begged, *why not forever?*
She said, *that's not how it works.*
She left him soon after for an Easy Answer.

Why me? cried Why.
He'd had some Easy Answers himself,
but they didn't satisfy.

He texted one of the Wherefores of Knocklyon,
they had a pint, made up their minds
that there were more questions than answers.

Building Castles

When I cut the grass
and twigs catch in the blades
the engine stops.

I know I should unplug
before I turn the body on its side,
before I take a risk.

I think of you:
our school excursion
to Bunmahon,

a dull day on the strand,
and you, one of the big girls,
say, let's make a sandcastle.

We kneel to face each other,
you unclip the leather band
of your prosthesis,

lay it down beside you,
its fingers curled,
a Bonsai hand fork;

you nudge and sweep the sand
with thumb and heel of hand,
while the other does the shaping.

I join in, unsure
of my two ordinary hands,
and listen to the story

of the lawnmower.
Does my mouth fall open
as you tell it

or am I old enough
to make believe
such stories sieve

through my ten fingers
every day,
are patted into place?

To Olga

You were the only girl on my wall
a *Jackie* centrefold, a forward split
across the torn-out staples.

At seventeen you back-flipped on the high bar,
back-tucked on the beam, you flew the floor
to bend like Slinky.

Circus-brave, you turned the world's head,
filled each girl's head
with Olympic gold.

I practised handstands, chalked my palms,
I scaled the rope to write your name
on the ceiling.

When you got a nine point eight
in the uneven bars, we all booed
the black-and-white Munich judges –

Give her Ten! In Montreal it was all
about Nadia, girls
and the world are fickle.

Nowadays you live in Arizona
drive a Subaru, teach kids
the Korbut Flip.

Someone called Alyssa posts
that you stole figs, tea, cheese and syrup.
A guy called Christian tells her she's unkind,

even Nixon told you, back when Belarussians didn't cry –
I have always been impressed with your ability
to land on your feet.

SHIPWRECKED

A Shipwreck Bag was a sack of supplies every Sunday –
bullseyes, fake cigarettes and spicy liquorice pipes,
pink or red beads on the bowl, like my dad's pipe,
which was filled and lit, smoked and re-lit,
smoked and emptied twenty times a day
to the sound of a rattling cough, copious spitting.

His thumb would be black,
his jacket pocket sometimes went on fire,
the Full Bent Cherry-Polished Pipe
left smoking away on its own.
He tapped and pulled and chewed on his pipe
and we tapped and pulled and chewed on ours.

In his sixties he gave it up, buried the pipe
under a rose bush at the Blackrock Clinic,
then closed his eyes as they bypassed his heart.
He developed a sweet tooth like ours,
tasted a handful of years with his mended heart.
But the cough rattled back, too late for a Shipwreck Bag.

GIFTS

The first time we were apart,
you rang from Dallas
full of news about the conference –
lunch with the lads at Hooters
served by busty waitresses.
Three artificial sunflowers
you brought back.

When your mum was fading,
we'd take turns
to brush plump petals
down her face,
to smooth her cheeks
with sunflowers,
yellow, purple, red.

Now the flowers bloom
beside our bed
with a soft dog you brought home
from a Scottish trip.
The real dog and I
permit you to tell stories,
fill our heads with Texan sunshine.

On Introducing my Husband to my Ex

I did not need to say to you,
darling, this is X,
the one who pumped my heart

with helium and cast it,
airborne to the whin,
where it lay punctured,

inhaling yellow,
no longer certain
what it was for;

and this, my love, is Y,
the one who landed my X
while I was still talking funny,

boosted and high.
So much time has passed
that we all feel safe

to come out again,
our adjusted hearts
vacuum-packed against

accidental damage,
but valiant,
curious and light.

The Best Thing about Hoovering

The neat new
Philips Hoover
hums me up
the narrow stairs,
sucks up all thoughts
but one:
the best thing
about hoovering
is that spring-loaded
moment when,
with deft bare toe to switch,
the whole long tail of it
retracts to spindle like a pack
of greyhounds in rewind,
that course and nudge
to form a single beast
careering backwards
to the start of time.

The worst thing
about hoovering
is fast-falling
from the landing
tangled in the hose,
wrong-footed by the trim,
head in the wrong place
below my feet;
hands lunging
for the hundred-year-old spindles
that can slip
or crack
or save;
my scream,
he tells me later,
is primeval,

prised from
the cave-woman
in my chest.

The best thing about falling
down the stairs
are the sounds
the dog and he make
as I bare my wounds:
a Passion of contralto
and bass-baritone,
a duet worthy
of the Lamentations
of the Prophet Jeremiah.

Dog Whisperer

He has taken to quoting
from Cesar Millan,
dog whisperer to the stars,
or at least to the dogs
of the stars.

It's all about nose,
then eyes, then ears,
as he sifts the dog's dinner
through his fingers,
folding it with his scent.

He practises the soft bite
on my shoulder,
forming a jaw with his hand,
restrains me as a bitch would her pups;
then practises on the hound.

He turns down the volume
on our favourite series
to nuzzle me gently,
stroke my back, remind me
to get inside the canine mind.

He tries out some whispering
during the ads,
some rehabilitation,
and Minnie does active submission
like she's read the book herself.

Be more like your dog,
he whispers: *forgive, take naps,*
fill your head with every new scent.
She is our Sirius, our summer,
our companion star.

Easter Sunday in IKEA and A&E

I was surprised how many people
choose IKEA for their Easter Sunday lunch.
That's where we are when they ring
to say your mum's been taken in.

Abandoning the Easter Sunday marzipan
and meatballs, we buy a Rutger swivel chair,
boxed up so neat we won't know till we're home
its legs are missing. In A&E

the Transfer Letter's been mislaid.
The pregnant doctor barks unanswerable questions
like *can you lift your legs*? Decides to do a reflex test,
applies a pointer to the patient's sole,

she kicks, squeals – *take the gun away*!
The doctor tries the other foot – *the gun! The gun!*
Well, says the doctor, *she can move her legs*.
Nothing can be done until the letter's found.

We pass the trolley hours with the IKEA catalogue,
admire a Manstad corner sofa bed with storage,
praise the finish on the Torsby dining tables.
Clutching a balled-up corner of her sheet

your mother polishes the pages. When we have read
and she has dusted every one, you start to sing.
At *Christ the Lord is Risen Today*
your mother moves her lips.

The lyrics are forgotten, so we hum *A Green Hill*
Far Away, repeatedly, until she sleeps.

Red Hen

We know nothing
about hens, yet find ourselves
in charge of half a dozen.

The odd girl out –
you call her Mrs One – loses
her footing in the mud.

You carry her
into the hen-house
with piano player hands.

Still there the next day,
she has turned her blunt
red beak to the wall.

We talk to neighbours
about red mites, infections,
wonder if she's egg-bound.

We fill her bowl
with cabbage-leaves,
stroke her tight wings.

Her sisters cry out,
foul her water,
shit on her plumage.

We are told you'd get
a new hen for the price
of the vet. For the first time

I want to crack a bird's neck.
Instead we hand her back,
ailing but alive.

Weeks later you find me
in quick tears
for the red hen;

you brush the rust
of my feathers, fill up
my hopper with oyster shells.

End of the Road

At the Applegreen in Enfield
there's a hearse pulled up.
Did the driver go in for a meal,

or a Crunchie, or did he stop
to GPS, to make enquiries?
Is he unfamiliar with Kilcock?

If so, has he been driving
round the country with a corpse,
feeling lost, which reminds me

of the life-sized torso
laid out bare in the boot
of my old Ford Focus,

its viscera dangling from hooks;
reminds me, too, that Murt's
dad was an undertaker,

how the men from other firms
would park and chit chat
in their limos outside church

but that was not the way of his dad
who would always go in,
who liked to stay close to his dead.

Sign at Crash Repair Garage, Penryn: 'Catalysts Tested'

Elbow to elbow on the Truro train,
I get engaged in conversation,

the kind of chat that happens
when you're squatting on a suitcase.

Hot smells of oil and diesel
remind me of the tantalizing offer

at a garage in Penryn:
'Catalysts tested'.

Can they determine your turning points,
instruct you in advance how

this chance meeting on the Truro train
could convert me so completely

that I'd look back years from now,
confirm – yes, that was the catalyst?

Or if the test of my encounter
read Catalytic Negative, would I

just scribble this guy's number
on the back of my hand, erase it later

with a twist of powdered soap
and burn away the chance?

Intuitives

You won't want to know
about the ghost
in your back bedroom,

or that someone jumped
from your first floor flat
onto thirteen granite steps.

Nor is it helpful, after the fact,
to learn the meanings
of numbers:

the icons for endings,
when together,
your lover and you

have succumbed to
a bungalow,
the finality of 9.

It serves no purpose
to know what's coming next:
yet after your lover has left

you'll take a lodger
who every single night
unwraps the Tarot;

you'll draw comfort
from its pentacles,
safety from its swords.

Fool's Credo

I could say that I believe
in the way a song dives behind my ribcage,
and stays there, pounding out its message
for the rest of my body to explain.

I could tell you I believe in the ten point plan,
or that I trust the hymnal, the tarot, the zafu
(on alternating days).

I could say I believe in the truth,
but you'd see through me, see that I'm no more
than an air picked up on the radio,
a transparent kneeling body,

yet the card I've picked reveals a zero,
shows a beggar ready on a precipice,
its message: *hold your nose and jump.*

Winnie-the-Pooh

To make things all right
he pulls the heavy hardback
from a dusty place.

Once upon a time,
a very long time ago,
about last Friday ...

In the voice reserved
for honey-hungry children
like Christopher Robin and me,

he reads of a craving
for sweetness, of blue balloons
deceiving the bees.

I like that the story
is told just for me, for the you
that is Christopher Robin

or anyone who listens;
told even for
this heffalumpen version

of a girl who heard it first
in the voice her mummy kept
for her kindergarten children,

for the fours and fives and sixes
who believed.

FORMAL APPLICATION

To be undivided must mean not knowing you are
– Jane Hirshfield

Now I am of age
I'd like to get in touch
with my Better Self.
Is she on file at the Department
of Alternative Selves?
Is there a form I can fill in?

Were we divided at birth
or did we rub together
in the same crib, bear
the same christening charms
before each was carried off
on separated ways?

Things being equal,
I want more than reunion;
my true goal
is to hand myself back,
step into her
immaculate groove,

her without-trying-
just-rightness.
I'll live in her,
moment after lucid moment
knowing who I was,
knowing that I am.

Autobiography

after Frank O'Hara

When I was a child,
I went by 'Jimmy';
fell from a high wall,
the arrow still in me.

My brother's underpants
with their boastful Y,
fresh from the hot press
I wore them all day.

To be a boy, to be a boy
was all I wanted;
girls set tables,
women waited.

And here I am:
moonstone, mascara;
despite myself, a woman,
mimicking O'Hara!

It Holds no Water

It is neither cup
nor jug nor demijohn
neither barrel nor bucket
nor basin nor butt
nor pitcher and ewer
nor firkin nor sump
nor bladder nor kettle
nor goblet nor flask
nor Waterford Glass
nor any other vessel
true to its task.

Your words fall through
the circles of your colander
the basket of your lies
the turlough of your almost-was
your net, your mesh
your gauze;
leave only the sticky
the stubborn, the scrap
your words fall through
– despite your dodging logic –
the unsealed gaps.

ENDING

There is a pleasure in finishing something,
like a roll of dental floss,
apparently everlasting but finally, not.

A novel – yes – that getting to the final page
that gives you all you were holding out for –
ties up, zooms out, or lets you down.

A bar of soap, a victory of sorts for frugality,
for not giving up as the final sliver
dives out of your hands,

has you bend more than once,
risk smacking your head, makes you follow
its last flat holding of juniper.

You may walk around for days, then,
almost remembering to buy more floss,
more soap, recalling the characters,

asking yourself why they did it,
was it really fair to expect you to buy it,
that fast, cheap ending?

But where is the pleasure in finishing this
once-beautiful thing, which is over, not
because no thread or words or fragrance remains,

but is wrapped up, wound down, folded
and closed because it's old or dusty
and has squandered its shine?

Dad's Canvassing Card

The year he went up for election
his photograph was printed in reverse:
the right side of his face on the left
the left side on the right.

His photograph was printed in reverse,
a mirror image of himself,
the left side on the right –
he looked like someone else.

A mirror image of himself:
his film star parting, that dimple,
he looked like someone else
with his *Houses! More Houses! Your Houses!*

His film star parting, that dimple,
you'd vote for those perfect blue eyes.
With his *Houses! More Houses! Your Houses!*
I don't know why he didn't win.

You'd vote for those perfect blue eyes,
but the right side of his face on the left?
I don't know why he didn't win
the year he went up for election.

BEST OF THREE

When it first came in, they'd use cigar box lids
for bats, a champagne cork for a ball.
They played it after dinner, as a parlour game,
the fathers back from India keeping score,
the uncles in their uniforms shaking hands.

Our dad taught us how to hold the blade,
coached us on how the sleight of hand required
to spin the ball depended on your stance,
your handshake grip, the flick of wood and rubber,
showed the three of us the chop, the loop, the kill.

Jack Frost was outside but we were holed up
round the table in the echoing house, and sweating.
Everyone played, even Uncle Arthur, whose hands
big as mill wheels dizzied and spun the spectators,
each grateful for the pipe smoke lightness of the ball.

Last night in the Parochial Lodge, my hands shook
as the ball danced away from me. New rules,
faster, up to eleven only and two serves each.
Slowly I corrected my footing as though
my father still stood by the net, score-keeping.

Come Quietly

And then
there are the poems
you shouldn't write,
poems out of uniform
flex crowbars
and flashlights;

secrets that will not
come quietly
are shackled
and coerced –
wary of the promises
that nobody gets hurt.

Walking our Dog to the Italian Coffee Shop

Her tail spins
at the speed of a Ferrari,

her ears are cones
of equilateral enquiry.

I take my coffee to a sunny bench
to write my diary

she lies beneath
and falls in love entirely

with the bare legs of men
from Cagliari.

Life Mask

If I'd been an Amsterdam merchant
I'd have had your features moulded;
mortared to the wall above
our third floor window on the Herengracht
so your nostrils of ceramic might inhale,
as long as these great buildings stood,
black pepper, cinnamon and cassia.

In years to come canal boat tourists,
lit up by The Yellow Sunflowers, thirsty
for the trickle from The Milkmaid's jug,
would marvel at your captain's nose,
those tulip lips, your perfect ears intact.
He never ate bread pudding,
they'd conjecture, *but he never lacked.*

EXECUTOR SALE

The ad said:
approx half an acre,
extensive, magnificent.

A gulp of magpies,
we peck our way
around an empty nest.

The agent has a crooked spine,
eyes of a sparrow hawk,
he flits from our path.

Inside, dark tongues
of floral wallpaper disclose
a smell of mould and must.

A square blue bottle
on the dining table:
Royal Salute Scotch Whiskey, 1801.

A panic button
in the master bedroom;
a cantilevered wheeling table;

depressions in the sand-pink carpet
where the bed's feet stood;
one mustard armchair.

They'll be sold,
jokes a magpie man,
as props for a film.

Here on the sideboard,
a funeral service sheet, inscribed:
With Christ which is far better.

The ad said:
approx half an acre,
extensive, magnificent.

With a View to Settling Down

Even though I've met you
three, four times,
we have never been alone together.

We touched, of course,
when the agent was engaged
on his phone,

I admired your solid back,
turned on your taps,
held your cold handles.

My warm heart
was rejected out of hand.
Months later, short of suitors,

you began to see me differently,
indulged me ... a rattan chair
in the gold-papered bedroom

where I could fall asleep,
my gaze on the grey-blue hammock
of the Irish Sea.

Today you are mine.
I drive all afternoon
to get to you,

misgivings
like ramps in the road,
prayers that we'll fall in love.

Presbytery Curtains

Like the threadbare carpet,
clapped-out cooker, we

are to be thrown in
with the house.

Far from this
our mitred corners.

Did we not pull our weight
for piety, security and insulation?

Far from this
our goblet pleats, our interlining.

All these years
we kept you artful and discreet.

Not once
did we swagger or rail,

not once reveal
the catch behind our nets.

Far from this
our custom finish.

Not for us
to draw conclusions.

Feedback

The reader who texted to say
she'd read the whole book at one sitting.

The reader who admitted
she only likes the sexy ones.

The man who simply said,
the thing is, my dad died too.

The reader who had lost a breast,
and was surprised to hear it spoken of.

The listener who confessed:
your work does nothing for me

on the page;
the listener who left.

The editor who emailed:
please send more.

The old friend who confides
at every public reading,

over the glass
of Lidl Chardonnay

God, I'm glad I never asked you out –
I'd hate to be in any of those poems.

Muses

Some time after I dropped off,
swaddled in an Autumn duvet,
a Foxford rug already fallen
on the leaf-strewn floor,

the skylight I'd left open
creaked in the breeze,
allowed in poem-flies,
mottled and fizzing

each carrying a word
on its poem-fly back.
They flitted and buzzed
until the room

was swarming
with their arrow selves,
implying, suggesting,
metaphorising, punching,

alliterating, dropping
flecks of pathos and bathos
on the blind as they left.
Late that afternoon,

dry and headachy,
I felt the room had changed –
the laptop I'd shut down
was awake again,

its insect hum
zinging the air.

—

WHO'S COUNTING?

(Bradshaw Books, 2010)

Months Before She Met Him

I

Yoga Class

I skipped my yoga class
because the man was due
to fix the curtain rail.

Upstairs, he poised in heavy boots
on the edge of my bed,
but not before prudently
peeling back the elegant blue
Brown Thomas duvet.

Beneath him I stood
at optimal angle to flaunt
my cleavage, to hand him screws.

Smoothly he inserted the rawl plug,
then with slightly quicker breath
he drove it deep
into my freshly painted, trembling
Orchid White walls.

Threading the hoops onto the pole
we lifted it together,
our fingers touching
as he tenderly
completed the work.

Later we did yoga together
dreamt up new asanas
and held them, and each other
until light began slinking through
my brand new curtains.

Ring Road

I had a date last night.

He was polite,
told me *all* about
the new Ring Road
which hasn't yet been built –
and his own new house,
which he's building, floor
by door
by floor.

But how could I concentrate
on the Lisbon Treaty, or the cost
of cement,
when the whole wide story of *your* heart
lies almost unknown to me?

If it had been *you*, sipping latte,
telling the placenames of your life,
I'd have hinged my eyes on the interval between
the cotton of your clothes
and your warm skin
and listened forever.

If only I could rest in that space
I suspect
that even the round ribbon
of ring roads waiting to be built
could cunningly
fill me
with wonder …

Txt Sex

Text messaging,
the first hot Sunday in May –
he: *I hope you're doing something*
wild. I'm
busy with lambing.
She: *Sun-bathing*
out the back,
does that count as wild?
He: *That depends*
on how naked you are ...

She pictures him delivering,
arm-deep
in placenta,
imagining her nakeder, fuller,
redder than she really is, outside
on a blue rug holding
a silver mobile phone.

She turns over, pale still,
unhooks her bra;
they joke about his sad life
chatting to sheep,
phone dating,
dreaming of nakedness
in Edenbrook Heights.

If she were less prudent,
she'd ask him over now,
shower him, sponge each finger carefully,
massage his neck and armpits
with apricot soap;
but it's not like that with them,
his wedding band has left a mark
that no lamb's blood can cover.

She dresses, texts goodbye
and phones
the take-away.

The Deer

Months before she met him
she was falling:
she'd seen his picture
in black and white,
Googled his life,
and heard
something of his reputation.

Months before she met him,
she knew,
she would drive headlong
to the earth's rim
just to see him live,
risking life and skin.

He was exactly as described:
a perfect, deep-throated
stag,
encircled
by dark-eyed, feisty does.

She knew,
as he unwrapped her heart,
that he was used to getting presents
like this;
even her breasts
stayed soft as he opened her,
confusing his hooves
with a skylark's wing.

Still later, as she combed his hair
with gratitude
– even though she'd always known –
it took everything she had

not to cry out
at the dark hair now covering her own arms
and her doe eyes reflected in his.

Months before she met him
she was falling.

THE PRISON OFFICER

After a spate
of bankers
called Frank,
and I.T. heads
(mostly Evan or Ivan or Keith),
it felt like progress
to meet P.J., a P.O.
from Westmeath.

P.J. had a soft face,
well-meaning,
and a soft hidden apron of flesh
beneath his navy fleece.
He had friendly hands,
and a deep rich melting chocolate voice –
she saved his messages
to play back over and over.

He told her about work,
the inmates, their rights:
to see a doctor every day;
to go to mass on Holy Days.
I think they have too many Holy Days
they should get rid of some of them
(by the way I like your hair –
do you dye it?)

After a spate
of bankers
called Frank –
who as good as asked her
how much she earned –
it was different, anyway,
to hear about prison:
the rec yard, the fights,

the being liked,
not being called a screw –
what could be rarer, she thought,
than to live half your life inside

and to like it.

Over to You

I haven't felt like making any sweeping statements
since I met you.

You haven't bowled me over,
knocked me over with a feather;
I'm neither overjoyed
nor overawed.

But overall,
I haven't overlooked
your overarching possibilities.

Let's say our lives have
overlapped, and not to overstate it:
I've overheard your thoughts –
discreetly overheating.

So why don't we get overdressed,
I'll overcook you dinner,
you'll oversimplify your oversized
life story.

You'll overreach out for my hand,
I'll overcast all caution to the wind,

the wind will coil around our voices,
overcome us, overcome us.

II

Skin Problem

Once some guy has climbed on you
grown on you, helped himself
to more of you,
nestled so nearly
under your skin
and then
abruptly
left

don't let it be said
you're an easily led,
easily lost,
misled, mislaid, mis-
ogynist-magnet

only
what do you do with
the bit of him that's left
under your thin,
middle-aged skin?

Single Mind

I want to know
how you do it.
Have you learnt to erase me
from your single mind
or does some part of it, a lip
or a sigh, persist.

I want to know
how your body forgets me.
If that curious circle
of shade around your navel
has no memory, then surely
the hundred nerve endings
of your middle finger
must hanker for my skin.

And if you won't tell me,
and if I can't touch you,
I will pursue the dull eraser
as you pursued me,
I will befriend the empty mind,
as my body is emptied,
I will espouse the soul's stillness

beyond you,
beyond me
beyond wanting.

Dear Life

Sometimes it's as though
we hold on for dear life.
Squeeze, cling, draw each other near,
the tighter the safer,
the warmer you enfold me
the harder it is to concede
that this holding on stands
between you and your dear god
and me and my dear life.

Hello Tina

He went to Dive School
for a week
on Inisturk.

Came back buoyed up
on oxygen, showed me
his Valsalva manoeuvre,
showed, like a toddler
mastering his letters,
his Underwater Plastic
Writing Slate,
on which stated
– dry as innocence –
'HELLO TINA'.

In the photos he wore
mask tank fins
eyes frog-like,
in the photos Tina
in neoprene wetsuit
looked unnecessarily slim.

'We're all going
to the Red Sea
at Easter, Tina
and her mate
have set it up.'

I decided there and then
to get serious, give me
a few weeks and I'd be
crazy about caverns,
a connoisseur
of Dead Man's Fingers,

an authority
on caves wrecks reeks.

Sink or snorkel
I would shimmy
with the darkness,
pioneer lost cities,
make friends
with bladderwrack
and giant clams
have the Great Whites eating
out of my hand.

III

The Spell

Instantly, you will know.
You will turn
from the book you will be reading
or the wood you will be turning
or the friend of a kind friend
who'll later introduce us.

There will be no crisis
of conversion,
since by then you will be dwelling
under clean slates, waiting
for the moment when
the collie at your heel
barks twice, makes eyes
at the collie at mine.

And in this version
of your certain future,
I will turn to you,
admire your dog's fine coat
and you will know, instantly.

Write Down Your Dreams, He Said

I dreamt about your kitchen,
the firm leather skin
of the year's first pumpkin
yielding under stainless steel.

I dreamt about your fingers at my sacrum,
fastening the strings of your Italian apron;
your lunar-grey eyes intent
on onions darkening in oil.

And I dreamt about my own
ice-cold-from-scraping-the-potatoes fingers,
tracing the bold muscles of your neck
for the very first time;

the vibration of your softening breath,
a taste of berries. All this,
and the euphoria of stillness,
I dreamt about, till finally sleep came.

Ambivalence

Your nearly-No
is so, so far
from my almost-Yes

that if I didn't
sort of
know you

I'd practically throw
my hat
at happiness.

Who's Counting?

You wore contact lenses
for the first three dates
French Connection shirts
your warm cheeks shaved.

You brought yellow daisies
on every second date
refilled my wine glass
after every second taste.

You played me Gershwin
braised me tofu
praised my textures
oiled my shoulders
wormed my compost
turned my corners

said you loved me
on the sixty-second date.

New Boyfriend's Party

I am not a diva,
my voice will not break windows
nor my deep dress dazzle your eyes.
I do not know the moves,
the notes, the nuances
that hurl a room
into a thirsty silence.

And when the people come,
instead of easing a path
between the unknown species,
I will hover too long
amongst the well-tilled borders
of my friends, or

finding foreign courage
will, clasping my machete,
slice needlessly
into the clinking air.

Until suddenly
I've left it too late
and they're all standing up
and making nodding noises

and we must meet soon
you must come to dinner
let's meet soon and chat
and lovely to meet you

and my sleep is filled
with the wise and witty things
I didn't say.

Instead
I am awake before you
counting bottles
dousing surfaces
raking cheesecake into sticky bins
raising damp napkins
from the crevices of seats

cooling my head
with the unworldliness of tea.

Good Friday Planting

I release my suitcase,
catch you shirtless, shaving,
clay and purpose
in your finger-nails,
a gold-ribboned egg
on the kitchen table.

First earlies,
your welcome home gift to me.
I'm away a week
and you're talking about
Red Dukes of York,
Charlottes, Edzell Blues,
the anticipated thrill
of lifting your first haulm.

I lift your fingers to my mouth,
taste phosphorus, potassium,
a trace of dibbled tubers;
savour the salty
afternoon drills of your chest.

Later, later we will feast
on Sharpe's Early Express.

Made To Measure

Does it make sense, any more,
to set it out in neatly raised beds?
To measure love with reference
to the earth's diameter,
the leagues between the poles,
the space between my sternum
and my spine? Does the old stuff
about the planets still apply?
Didn't Shakespeare cover all that?

Should we not talk of love
in terms of kilojoules?
Combine our circuit boards,
get close in mega-pixels?
In the new century
do we not calculate intensity
in coloured dots?
Make love in dpi?

But still there is the precious gap
between this afternoon and now,
the dip and dive of swallows
on a green road hemmed by fuschia.
Your camera describes foxgloves,
flag iris, teasel and me;
and between Bull's Head
and Knocknadobar
there is yet space for us
that can't be counted.

Dream Wedding

We had chilli ramen last night,
a satay sauce, a burgundy
too sturdy for my stomach.

Aer Lingus had a sale till midnight
so we put our money down
– red kisses at the keyboard –
New England honeymoon.

I dreamt about a woman
at our wedding; yellow noodles
dangled from her mouth,
you smiled at her
and flicked them away
with your tongue.

In the dream I roared at you,
demanded nothing less
than all my money back.

This morning when I told you,
smooth-shaven, hot press fresh,
you just kissed me softly and said –
no noodles at our wedding.

THE SMEARS OF THE WORLD

Gardener

for my father

Tonight my house is bursting with sympathetic flowers:
crinkled white carnations
upright in every vase;
baby's breath exhaling from the glasses;
lilies filling every jug.

I want to repaint all the walls magenta,
the doors cerulean blue,
buy daffodils to launch spring early,
replace every gerbera and freesia,
every sober eskimo rose.

At least you got to see the snowdrops
I carried to your bedside
in wicker baskets cushioned with moss
(Protestant flowers, my cousin said).

But all the colours that you planted
wait still, biding their time
in company with you
under winter's desolate garden.

Metastasis

In his last weeks
he sends a dozen letters,
makes recompense,
receives his friends,
talks, tires, takes tablets,
holds each person near.

The house itself
has folded in its corners,
walls warm and soften
to accommodate his waning,
medicine gets stronger,
death is just behind him
and he starts to slip,
spits blood,
has the bishop pray
above his head.

In his last days
he is stoned on morphine,
grins wide-eyed at the high of it;
then there is only sleep.
Time stretched with concern
for his poor body,
turning him,
moistening his tongue,
oiling his dried lips,
scenting the room
with lavender and rosemary.

In his last moments
there is just my father;
his gasps,
each vying
not to be the last one;

and we three women,
sharing his hands
and brow between us,
talking him through,
sending him on,
in spite of us.

REMEMBRANCE

On Christmas Eve morning
my mother crafts three wreaths
for the recent dead.

At the last one, my father's,
she sinks holly and chrysanthemums
in a ring of quicksand.

We bear them like frankincense
silent down Maudlin Street, oasis
suckling our finger-tips;

I unlock the church gate
lean over
freshly-cut stone.

From over the road, outside Langton's
– even as we whisper our greetings –
flies a loaded taunt:
'She's a fine arse – for a Protestant!'

Washing Dishes for my Mother

Uncovered,
the tight-bound, spring-coloured heart
of a butterhead lettuce,

one of the last things on earth
I can offer you.

I clatter dishes,
you wait in the half-dark
for a supper that will not sustain you.

Later, hands drop
into grateful water,
wishing these dishes would continue forever.

If this
were all that was left to me
it would contain me:

my hands
on your plate and cup
in a moss-green basin

purposeful,
wiping away
the smears of the world.

Before Cancer

I don't want to think of you
hopeless on a metal bed,
choice ebbing from your limbs.

I want to remember you industrious,
baking meringues first thing
on a Saturday morning.

I don't want to think of you immobile,
terrified of forfeiting everything.

I want to remember you electric,
wagging a finger, censorious,
'Oh Shir, you're such a mimic!'

I need to conjure you sure-footed,
threading a path between sycamores,
harvesting loganberries,
saving dried quinces on a Spanish plate.

I need to think of you before metastasis,
Tamoxifen and Dexamethasone
became your daily bread.

Instead I am suspended
in a February morning,

bringing you a cupful of snow
from the hospital car-park,
holding your strong left hand,

ice fading
in our fingers.

Calling to Me Through the Woods

I have gone out searching for you
in amongst the thick-knit spruces
at the place where the fire-break peters
in the hours when birds sleep
and long-boned alsations crouch
alongside last night's bonfire.

I have carried no torch
for fear of waking the living
just bluebells
and foxgloves and rosemary
and the torn part of me that aches
for your stout-hearted stillness.

But you are in hiding
fastened with the moss, maybe,
to the river wall,
upstanding with the heron
or endurance swimming
with the wisest salmon
back bravely to the dark Atlantic salt.

Sustainable Dying

Wrap me in sack-cloth
and bury me under
our Guaranteed Irish
permaculture plot.

Let no formaldehyde
sully my creases
but bathe me in organic
Fair Trade frankincense.

I'll forgo cremation –
my previous first option –
since it's such a frittering
of priceless fuel.

Plant me under blackberries
and when your lips grow dark
be in no doubt –
I gave you sweetness.

Exact Science

On Christmas Eve
he draws it all out
on the page.

The senior surgeon,
red-eyed from poring over
wayward stars,
makes no bones about
calling a sign a sign.

Prince of the modern Magi
he lays out his thesis,
antithesis, then erases both:

Of course
it's your own decision.

MASTECTOMY

You get given
certain things in twos –

love-birds, book-ends,
matching china tea mugs –

and even though
on any given morning

it is all you even think of
to hook one fine china

top designer
duck-blue tea-mug

from your dry beech
draining rack

to boil and pour and stir
and watch Darjeeling towers spiral;

there are still the days
when there is company for breakfast,

and on these fine mornings
let me tell you

it is good to know
that there are two

extra special, same but different
unchipped breakfast blue mugs

made to grace
your table.

Menopause

She's been loitering,
squeezing by
in soft-tailored XL suits,
her hints at wisdom,
promises of power
disguising her shape.

I meet her in the shower,
free-falling breasts
lounge across the creases
of her belly. She teases me,
cries *nonsense, clinging*
to the cramping calendar of youth
when freedom is at hand.

And now some magic pill's
going to catapult me
forward in years, high-speed me
pouting and railing
to the palace of the crone;
sweat me, dry me, whisper me
the secrets, make me *mature*
before my time.

Reconstructed

At her kitchen table
in the stark morning
of New Year's day,
a woman I've just met
spreads marmalade
on toasted soda bread,
recounts the ins and outs
of losing both her breasts.

Before I know it
in her keenness
to prepare me
as no doctor could,
she is pushing aside
cups and crumbs,
pulling wool and cotton
up over her ribs,
straining to unhook
her hospital-white bra.

Faced with the tender
drumlins of her chest,
each raked with
a flat red seam,
I am swept away
that it is she
who is consoling me,
her wise heart
which has remained
inviolate.

The Fitting

With dressmakers' measure
the stylish surgeon
sizes up my breast.

Her buffed and polished fingers
range and dart from rib to nipple
she whispers numbers,
fourteen, seven, seven.

Practised hands
flick through a catalogue,
select a replica
to get me even.

We talk wedding plans
the dress, the date,
she counsels on décolletage.

Next month, she will cut
and stretch and boost and stitch,
fit for my wedding day,
make me a match.

Waiting List

The new breast
is always fridge-cool.

Hot-palm its pleats
it is teen-pert,
bra-perfect,
soap-stone round.

Tracked across
the almost-centre,
puffy-concertinaed
where they sewed it up,
a fist's width
below the oxter.

Still nippleless,
I am a polished moonstone
lady-in-waiting.

BREAD & BUTTER

Cinnamon

A trendy, chi chi,
old-style, new-style cafe,
Queen's Park, London,

savouring my two best friends
like morning buns
like melted yellow butter
drizzled over hungry tongues

enabled by the secrets of Lavazza,
smooth sticks of Madagascar,

to tell everything we know
whisper everything we feel
– no spice spared.

Bus Fellows (Spain 1990)

He speaks without teeth –
he must be sixty –
in a language I don't quite remember,
something about my throat
and a lorry load of goats
awaiting him in Ronda.

Clamped between him
and the coach window
his elbow niggles my side
and sticky hands
fiddle with his fly.

He woos without teeth
in the universal language of intrusion.
I spit back – definitely – NO!
but conjure up,
should there be any room for doubt,
a lorry load of husbands
awaiting me in Ronda.

€UROGREEN

Hand-sewn hemp intimates
from Kathmandu,

sasawashi suits are made-to-measure,

mud baths in Bad Kissingen
skilleted tofu,

she's eco-chic, she's über-clean
she's green forever.

Frocks dyed with fraughans
from Mullaghcleevaun,

water is lab-tested as a rule,

exfoliates with sea-salt
has her eye-brows drawn,

she's eco-chic, she's über-clean
she's no green fool.

Sponsored trees in São Luís,
Minke whales in Mull,

offset a mini-break in Nîmes,

her euros may be green, darling,
but life is never dull,

she's eco-chic, she's über-clean
forever green.

Travelling Companions Wanted

Bearded, serene
ornithologist, Assisi,
seeks fellow travellers
(preferably male)
for wildlife safari.
First Aid a bonus.
May have problems
with bleeding.

Contact: Francesco

Fun-loving,
original fruitarian, female,
seeks man for city breaks,
naturism, anywhere
but gardens.
Snake phobia.

Contact: Eve.

German woman, blonde,
long hair to die for,
seeks well-connected guy
for abseiling, fun times,
will make it worth your while,
will teach you
the secret of stillness
if you can just get me
out of here.

Contact: Rapunzel

Likely lad, UK,
seeks mates, up
for a bit of mullarkey,

must have martial arts
and sprint fast
at high altitudes.
Best blokes get nest-eggs
like what you've never seen.

Contact: Jack

Not Coffee

I want my coffee to be
brisk and rich and muscular.

I want my coffee
to nuzzle me awake,
a tongue of brightness
filtered through my bedroom window.

I want my coffee sonorous,
to call my name from cafe terraces,
mosaic tables shaded from the midday sun.

I want my coffee ceremonial,
a daily Event.

I am trying to adjust to Dandelion,
to its flat, thin sweetness,

loath to admit it's the bitterness I miss.

For Rachael

You have evolved
from scattiest girl
to junior baker.

You measure flour and sugar,
know with the confident alchemy of cooks
to omit the baking powder.

You crack an egg and giggle
at the one long line
formed in its side.

I only use eggs,
you tell me,
from Woodville Farm.

At almost twelve
you have become your mother
thirty-two years ago

piling moist ginger snaps,
banana bread and carrot cake
into the sweet-toothed mouth of the Aga.

Then as now
I looked on, made myself useless
to the best of my ability.

Until recently
it looked like you took after me,
haphazard middle child –

I must not begrudge you
a clatter of your mother's talents;
bake on, sweet niece,

keep a little for me.

Half-way Home

It was a live-in situation
at the Liverpool hostel
for homeless men.
For full board
and twenty quid a month
I mopped floors, played pool,
changed urine-soaked sheets,
wheeled Mikey to the pub
on a Wednesday, after the pension.

He asked me awkward questions
about marriage, sobbed when I said
it wasn't in my plans, 'But
did your mother not explain?'
Once or twice he threw me
a hundred pounds,
which had been mouldering
under his mattress.

The cook had cystitis,
she said I was the fattest vegetarian
she'd ever seen. Tommy
was on hormone treatment
for a female to male sex change,
and Billy held his yellow-grey head
as he paced, 'Rainhill,
Rainhill is my home,
Rainhill, Rainhill, Rainhill
is my home.'

On Christmas Day there was beer
and cigarettes and crackers,
I sneaked my boyfriend in
and we lay listening
in my attic room:

Oh come all ye faithful,
Joyful and triumphant,
Rainhill, Rainhill,
Rainhill is my home.

(Rainhill: the psychiatric hospital in Liverpool)

Acknowledgements

As well as previously uncollected poems, *Origami Doll: New and Collected Poems* includes the following collections: *Stone Dress* (Arlen House, 2015) and *Who's Counting?* (Bradshaw Books, 2010).

Grateful acknowledgement is made to the following publications for poems that appeared in them, sometimes in a different form: *Washing Windows: Irish Women Write Poetry* (Arlen House anthology); *Clifden 35; Clockhouse; Five; In Touch* magazine; *Interpreter's House; Kind of a Hurricane; Listowel Writers' Week Anthology 2014; Orbis; Salzburg Review; Signal Arts Magazine; Stand Magazine; The Muse; These Things Happen: Writings from Bray Active Retirement Association; Poetry Life, The SHOp, The Stinging Fly, Bray Arts Club Journal, Galway Now, The Works, Revival, Boyne Berries, The Space Inside, Tributaries, Cyphers, Gates of Ivory and Horn* (Airfield Writers' anthology), *Shape Sifting* (Cinnamon Press Anthology); *Poetry Ireland Review.*

A version of 'The Dog Whisperer' was chosen for outdoor display by North West Words Poetry for Spaces, Donegal.

'On Introducing my Husband to my Ex' was shortlisted for the Strokestown International Poetry Prize in 2012.

A version of 'Executor Sale' won first prize in Listowel Writers' Week Originals Single Poem competition, 2014.

'Stone Dress' won the PENfro Poetry Competition 2015.

Shirley McClure's translation of 'Midnight' by Gabriela Mistral was published in Marie Heaney (ed), *All Through the Night: Night Poems & Lullabies* (Poetry Ireland, 2016).

About the Author

Shirley McClure was born in Waterford in 1962. She attended Newtown School, studied English Literature and Spanish in Trinity College Dublin and undertook a Master's degree in Latin-American Studies at Liverpool University. She worked as a natural health practitioner, practising and teaching shiatsu and aromatherapy. She also taught creative writing with a particular interest in writing and health.

She wrote her first poems when she was eight, encouraged by her teacher parents and artist grandmother. She continued to write sporadically for many years, but began to take her poetry seriously upon prompting by close friends on her fortieth birthday. Eight years later her first collection, *Who's Counting?* was published by Bradshaw Books in 2010, having won the *Cork Literary Review's* Manuscript Competition 2009. *Spanish Affair,* her CD of poems and music, was launched in 2015, with proceeds going to Arklow Cancer Support where she ran a writers' group. Her second collection, *Stone Dress,* was published in August 2015 by Arlen House.

Her poetry was widely published in literary journals and she won numerous awards, including Listowel Writers' Week Originals Poetry Competition 2014, the PENfro Poetry Competition 2015 and runner-up in the Patrick Kavanagh Award 2009. Shirley enjoyed residencies at the Tyrone Guthrie Centre, Annaghmakerrig, the Heinrich Böll Cottage, Achill Island, Ty Newydd Creative Writing Centre, Wales and Key West Literary Seminar. She lived in Bray, Co. Wicklow with her husband, Philip Beck, and their dog, Minnie.